I0760077

NORTH WEST RAILWAYS GALLERY

A PICTORIAL JOURNEY THROUGH TIME

In celebration of the 90th Anniversary of the Manchester Locomotive Society and in remembrance of the many members who have bequeathed their photographic collections to the Society over many years.

This book is dedicated in particular to Eddie Johnson, Member No.412, who joined in 1961 and after many years lapsed, rejoined in 1997 and died 6 December 2024. He provided much of the information about the photographers in this book

Front cover photo: Lancashire & Yorkshire Railway's pioneer Dreadnought 1506 of 1908 leaving Sowerby Bridge with a Manchester–Halifax–Leeds & Bradford train, c1920. (Manchester Locomotive Society Collection)

Back cover photo: Unrebuilt 'Royal Scot' 46156 *The South Wales Borderer* passing Cheadle Hulme with a Manchester London Road–Euston via Wilmslow and Crewe express, c1952. (Tom Lewis/Manchester Locomotive Society Collection)

NORTH WEST RAILWAYS GALLERY

A PICTORIAL JOURNEY THROUGH TIME

DAVID MAIDMENT

AN IMPRINT OF PEN & SWORD BOOKS LTD.
YORKSHIRE – PHILADELPHIA

All David Maidment's royalties from this book with the permission and support of the Manchester Locomotive Society will be donated to the Railway Children charity [reg. no. 1058991] [www.railwaychildren.org.uk]

First published in Great Britain in 2025 by
Pen and Sword Transport
An imprint of
Pen & Sword Books Ltd.
Yorkshire - Philadelphia

ISBN 978 1 03613 843 1

A CIP catalogue record for this book is available from the British Library.

Typeset by SJmagic DESIGN SERVICES, India.

The Publisher's authorised representative in the EU for product safety is
Authorised Rep Compliance Ltd., Ground Floor, 71 Lower Baggot Street, Dublin D02 P593, Ireland.
www.arccompliance.com

For a complete list of Pen & Sword titles please contact

PEN & SWORD BOOKS LIMITED
George House, Beevor Street, Off Pontefract Road, Hoyle Mill,
Barnsley, South Yorkshire, England, S71 1HN.
E-mail: enquiries@pen-and-sword.co.uk
Website: www.pen-and-sword.co.uk

or

PEN AND SWORD BOOKS
1950 Lawrence Rd, Havertown, PA 19083, USA
E-mail: uspen-and-sword@casematepublishers.com
Website: www.penandswordbooks.com

THE MANCHESTER LOCOMOTIVE SOCIETY – 90 YEARS ANNIVERSARY & ACKNOWLEDGEMENTS

The Manchester Locomotive Society (MLS) was formed in 1935 at a meeting held in Manchester Mayfield station on 6 December. Nineteen local railway enthusiasts attended and became the founder members. Its objective: 'To provide an organisation centred on Manchester for the study and discussion of the historical, engineering and operating aspects of Locomotives and Railways and to provide facilities and activities of interest to Railway Enthusiasts.' Its first organised trip was to Crewe Works, Crewe North and Crewe South sheds on 1 January 1936. In 1955 it acquired its own meeting room in an old parcels office at Manchester Central station. When that station closed, it moved to the former Stationmaster's office at Sale until that line was converted to a Metrolink tram line in 1992. It then moved to three rooms on the first floor of the station offices at Stockport, accommodation that has now grown to eleven rooms. Membership peaked at 180 in the 1950s, dropped to around 100 at the end of steam but currently has a record 220 members.

I have been a member of the Manchester Locomotive Society since 2013 and have been indebted to the Society for the copious use of its comprehensive library for research purposes and its prolific collection of railway photographs for illustrating the thirty-four books written by me already published or in the process of publication by Pen and Sword Ltd. This book about railways and their trains in the North West is illustrated entirely by photographs from the archives of the Society, mostly previously unpublished, the vast majority of which were taken by members of the Society during the previous ninety years. The photographs have been selected by me with advice and support from the MLS's photograph archivist, Paul Shackcloth and its membership secretary, Chris Tasker, who, with the late Eddie Johnson, a long-term Society member, have given further details for the photo captions and the vignettes of the key photographers who not only provided many images for this book, but many also for my previous Pen & Sword books.

I am very grateful for the support given by the Society and its members to the Railway Children charity (www.railwaychildren.org.uk) which I founded in 1995 to protect, support and rehabilitate the thousands of street living and runaway children found on the transport systems of the world in over ten countries during the last thirty years, and currently concentrated in India, East Africa and not forgetting in the UK itself. The MLS has generously allowed me to scan and use its photographs free of any publication fee as

I donate all the royalties to the charity and this fact has meant that I have been able to profusely illustrate all my books without worrying about the costs eating into the royalty sums.

The Society's clubrooms which house the library and photograph archives are located above the station buildings on platforms 1 & 2 of Stockport station and are open every Wednesday for research and development purposes and at other times for illustrated lectures published on their website, www.manlocosoc.co.uk and in the Society's bi-monthly magazine, *The Mancunian.*

As I stated earlier, many of the MLS archived photographs have been taken by previous Society members, and I pen below a few details about some of those photographers who were the most prolific and who feature in the captions of the illustrations in this and other books of mine. I start with a couple who were founder members of the Society ninety years ago.

Harold D. Bowtell

Member No.1, joined 6 December 1935, died 3 February 1999.

Harold was a railway scholar, with a specialist interest in reservoir railways, and one published book, *A History of the Lancaster & Carlisle Railway.* He was a confirmed bachelor, lived initially in Bury and later near Kendal overlooking the West Coast main line. He worked in Manchester in the insurance industry, with boiler insurance being his main area of expertise. He was a captain in the Royal Engineers in the Second World War and spent time in India where he enjoyed access to the footplate of Indian steam locomotives. He owned a Leica 35mm camera.

Neville Fields

Member No.2, joined 6 December 1935, died 29 July 2010.

Another founder member, one of a handful of teenage boys who were the initial club members. He served in the RAF in South Africa during the war and took part in the government scheme of training ex-servicemen for teaching posts on their return to civilian life. He became Assistant Head Teacher at a school in Stockport, and was a councillor for the Heald Green area, becoming Lord Mayor of Stockport in the 1980s. He used a Rolliflex camera.

George Martin Shoults

Member No.37, joined May 1936, died 20 November 1975.

George was a founder member and past President, and was taking railway photographs well before the MLS started, particularly in Scotland around Aberdour in 1910/11 and in the Chorlton area of Manchester in 1913. During the Second World War he was captured by the Italians and spent most of it as a prisoner of war. His son, Charlie, Member No.40, also took railway photographs but was primarily interested in modelling.

J. Doug Darby

Member No.58. joined January 1937, died 15 July 2009.

Doug was an Industrial Chemist working for the Carborundum Company at Trafford Park. He spent some time working in Australia and also in India. He befriended Ronnie Gee, both joining the Society around the same time, eventually becoming its President. He used a Zeiss Ikonta camera. He died aged 92, bequeathing his photo and book collection to Ronnie Gee, who in turn left them to the MLS library and photo archive.

William Whitworth

Member No.72, joined March 1937.

Was a dentist and a prolific photographer especially in the Crewe area. He took many photos at Crewe North shed with the 'sleeper fence' as background – so many in fact that the wall was nicknamed 'Whitty's Wall'. He was friendly with the Crewe North Shedmaster and was given access to a small shed at the depot for his photographic activities there. He died 21 April 1957.

Bill Potter

Member No.115, joined January 1940, resigned, May 1993.

Bill was an early member of the Society and the archive has many of his photographs of excellent quality taken in the 1930s and 1940s. He lived in Burnage and worked for Smith's Instruments who designed and constructed instruments for the RAF including such plane equipment as altimeters. He moved to Cheltenham in the war and lived in a house owned by the company. Unfortunately when Smith's Instruments were bought by another company they sold all their property leaving Bill and his wife homeless, a sad experience in his retirement. His photographic collection is now with the Kidderminster Railway Museum archive.

Ronnie Gee

Member No.137, joined April 1943, died 6 December 2016.

Ronnie was a lifelong railwayman starting as a Longsight fitter in 1943, but because of his asthma, had to leave the shed environment and became a booking lad at Guide Bridge. He joined the MLS in 1943 as well, and finished his railway career as a Station Inspector covering both Stockport and Macclesfield. He earned the nickname 'Chaos' as when railway problems arose he always seemed to be on duty and in the thick of it! He was a fervent Manxman and his other main passions were railways and the Book of Common Prayer – he was involved with Manchester Cathedral. He started his photographic career with a Box camera, advanced to a Rollicord , finishing with a Zeiss Ikonta and an Olympus. He was meticulous in documenting captions for his photographs, an example that unfortunately few followed.

Alan Gilbert

Member No.150, joined October 1945, died 1 September 2014.

Another confirmed bachelor, he held a very senior post as Chief Accountant for Granada TV. He lived in Cheadle Hulme and was Treasurer of the MLS for 51 years and was a past President. He travelled widely with the LGCB tours to Europe and other overseas railways and had a large (and expensive) collection of cameras including a Hasselblad, a Nikon 35mm and a 16mm camera. He was involved with the Anglican church in Cheadle Hulme and left a large legacy to both the church and the Society. Visitors to his house observed that an opened copy of the *Financial Times* was always prominent on his table!

Norman Harrop

Member No.164, joined March 1946, died 28 May 2012.

Norman was a cousin of Gerald Harrop, one of the Society's founders and Member No.3. In addition to his work of locomotive portraits on shed, he was a prolific photographer on the lineside, taking both black and white, and from 1957, colour slides. He was the Sales Manager of the family meat firm and as such, had a car in which he travelled on both business and railway photography all over the country, but particularly in his home area, Stockport. He often took fellow MLS members Peter Ward and John Spencer with him. Many of his colour slides were published in a 'Silver Link' publication, *British Steam in Colour, 1957-1975.* He was a Committee Member of the Bahamas Locomotive Society when 5596 was purchased from BR in 1967.

Neville Knight

Member No.202, joined 1950, died 25 December 2016.

Neville was a transport enthusiast photographing buses as well as a railways, his main focus being transport in the North West. He was an electrician and wired the MLS clubrooms at Stockport in 1996 when they took over the former derelict rooms on Stockport station. He was widowed and remarried.

Brian K.B.Green

Member No.212, joined January 1951, resigned January 2015.

A railwayman who started his career as a clerk at Liverpool Street in 1947, he moved to Manchester working for the LNER Goods Manager at London Road, then at Reddish Electric depot until it closed, when he left the railway to be an AA switchboard operator. His railway photographic work included extensive use of his photos for the Ian Allan ABC locospotter books, many taken on his frequent shed and Works visits – he claimed he had seen every active steam locomotive owned by British Railways! He was the MLS librarian for many years, used a Rolliflex, then a Nikon 35mm camera. His vast collection was sold to another member, Norman Preedy, who bequeathed it to the Kidderminster Railway Museum archive. He married somewhat late in life, but suffered poor health in his latter days.

Jim Davenport

Member No.218, joined March 1951, died 24 August 1998.

A railwayman, starting at Lees shed near Oldham. He was another railway bachelor, and close friend of another member, Peter Hutchinson whom he often accompanied on railway photographic jaunts. He frequented in particular the Diggle route between Stalybridge and Huddersfield, but was a prolific photographer worldwide.

Peter Hutchinson

Member No.219, joined March 1951, died 10 August 2009.

He was a draughtsman at Ferranti's in Oldham and did a lot of railway photographic work on the Continent as well as accompanying Jim Davenport on photographic ventures in the UK. He also took many shots in the Crewe and Skelton Junction areas. He, like Ronnie Gee, was meticulous in inscribing in detail the captions on his prints including the details of the camera settings used.

Tom Lewis

Member No.303, joined January 1954, died 19 October 1971.

Tom lived in Cheadle Hulme, was married and had a son, David, who was also a railway photographer. Much of his work was on 6cm x 9cm glass plates and covered much of the West Coast Main line between Stafford and Warrington in the first half of the 1950s. He died of a rare blood disorder, leaving his collection to Nobby Clark, a railway fireman, who loaned some of it out, but unfortunately much then went missing. The remaining collection is held in the Kidderminster Railway Museum archive.

Ray Farrell

Member No.643, joined July 2008, died 26 February 2016.

Ray was born in 1934 in Bury, was married with one daughter. He was very involved in sports and local social activities, being the founder member, treasurer, secretary and president of the Elton Football Club for 38 years and president of the Elton Fold Working Men's club for 22 years. He was an accountant for various businesses, ending as Managing Director of the Hollas Group. He was a member of the East Lancs Preservation Society. had lineside photographic permits for the Leeds ER area and the West Coast main line, in particular between Wigan and Preston. He was the author of a book on the Wigan–Preston line published in 2007.

A number of other Society members were primarily railway photograph collectors who made their collections available to the MLS archive. These included Jim Peden, John Hilton, Bob Miller, David Young and Mike Bentley. Bob was a specialist on the Cheshire Lines Committee railway and has written books on this and also co-wrote a book on the Cambrian Railways. He had a large collection of early Great Western locomotive photos including Broad Gauge subjects on which I have drawn for my Pen & Sword GW books. Mike has a huge collection which has been made available to me also for many of my Pen & Sword books, especially Great Western in the Birmingham area, Great Central, LNER and LMS subjects. He was a locomotive driver at Buxton until injured by a slab of concrete thrown at his train by a vandal smashing the windscreen of his diesel locomotive – he still lives in Buxton and offers his photographic collection if the MLS archive cannot suffice. David Young was another collector and member who died last year and the Society is currently cataloguing his photos, mainly BR LMR subjects, and inserting them in the MLS archive. One photographer whose work is used frequently in this book was a non-member, E.R. Morten, but his son John loaned his negatives to the Society, which Paul Shackcloth then printed for the use of Society members.

All photographs in the book are from the Manchester Locomotive Society Collection. Where the name of the photographer is known, that is shown within the caption. If the photographer was a Society member, I will use their Christian name in the photo credit. However, many of the photographs in the collection bear no photographer or copyright details and if I have missed acknowledging any other photographer please contact the publisher.

I also wish to thank the Pen & Sword Commissioning Editor, John Scott-Morgan and the Transport theme Production Manager, Janet Brookes, for their help and support and the whole production team for the quality and timeliness of the publication of the book in their Gallery series.

David Maidment
MLS Member No.712, joined 2013.
Founder Ambassador, Railway Children charity

Retired Head of Safety Policy, British Rail & former Chief Operating Manager, London Midland Region.

Chris Tasker, the late Eddie Johnson and Paul Shackcloth against a background of some of the railway memorabilia owned by the club, November 2024. This photo was taken during Eddie's last visit to the MLS clubrooms. (David Maidment)

The entrance to one of the clubrooms of the Manchester Locomotive Society with memorabilia including a couple of 'Jubilee' nameplates and other 'essentials' staple to the club members' existence! (David Maidment)

Another view of the main MLS clubroom with two members assisting Paul Shackcloth to catalogue photographs recently donated to the club. The memorabilia on view include nameplates donated by members, including *Shrewsbury* removed from a GW 'Badminton' 4-4-0, No.4115, in 1927 when the management decided to remove place names to avoid confusion for their passengers and *City of Manchester,* not from the LMS Pacific of that name, but the Great Central class '1' 4-6-0, No.425, LNER B2/B19, withdrawn in 1947. (David Maidment)

INTRODUCTION

The area covered by the photographs defined by me as the 'North West' runs from Shrewsbury, Birkenhead, Colwyn Bay, Liverpool and Fleetwood in the West, to Huddersfield, Halifax, Woodhead and Peak Forest in the East; and from Stafford in the South to Tebay and Shap in the North. The majority of the photographs are concentrated around the homes of the key MLS photographers in the area bounded by Preston, Manchester, Stockport and Crewe. Locomotives and locations come from the Lancashire and Yorkshire, London & North Western, London Midland & Scottish Railways and the BR London Midland Region in the main, with a scattering from the Great Western and Midland Railways and in the most recent times, from the Virgin, Northern, EWS and other train operating companies. The photographs start with some of the most significant stations in the North West and are then arranged as a journey through time from the later years of the Victorian era, through the Edwardian and Inter-war years, the last flourishing of steam power of British Railways in the 1950s and '60s, and the proliferation of diesel and electric power from the 1960s through to the current era.

The earliest photographs feature the locomotives of the LNWR's Francis Webb and the L&Y's John Aspinall and these companies' trains dominate the photographs taken before the Grouping in 1923. Although steam power was the driving force for passenger and freight traffic throughout that period, both the LNWR and the L&Y had taken the first steps towards electrification as early as 1904 with the opening of the Liverpool–Southport four-rail system in 1904, followed by an experiment with the DC overhead system in 1913 and electrification from Manchester to Bury with a third rail system in 1913. The LNWR also invested in electrification for its suburban railway, but in the London area rather than the North West.

George Whale and Bowen Cooke followed Webb and chose robust simple 4-4-0 and 4-6-0 engines rather than developing Webb's complex compound locomotives and George Hughes introduced his heavy 'Dreadnought' 4-6-0s in the first decade of the twentieth century and continued a new strain after the First World War, not completing them until after the formation of the LMS. The new LMS locomotive department had a somewhat turbulent early period as managers from the former Midland Railway held key positions in the new company and clashed with the policies of the former L&Y and LNWR in particular. The heavy but less frequent West Coast expresses were underpowered by Midland Compounds and their LMS built version supplementing the LNWR 'Claughtons' and 'George V' 4-4-0s until Fowler hurriedly ordered the three-cylinder 'Royal Scots' from the North British Company in 1927.

William Stanier came from the Great Western in 1932 and quickly saw the dual needs of healing the rifts in the motive power management of the company and the provision of higher powered locomotives that could form a more standardised fleet on the lines that he had learned from the GW's Churchward and Collett. The 1930s saw the era of the streamlined expresses with the Boards of the LNER and LMS vying with each other, which Stanier recognised in the production of his 'Princess Coronation' pacifics in 1937, but had concentrated his skills and those of the team he built around him in the design and construction of the 'Black Fives', the 'Jubilees', the 8F 2-8-0s, and his 2-6-4 tanks, all built in quantity to support the pacifics, and used widely all over the system, replacing many of the L&Y and LNWR locomotives in the North West.

G.A. Ivatt continued the standardising work in the post-war years and the LMS motive power management including E.S. Cox and Robert Riddles became leading forces in the development and introduction of the BR standard classes. Many of these found activity in the North West, especially in the closing stages of steam operation when the remaining Britannias were drafted to Crewe and Carlisle Kingmoor from their Eastern, Western and Scottish Region depots, joining 70030-70034 which had been allocated to Longsight from their construction and 70043-70049 which were allocated to the LM Region later.

The first sign of the motive power policy of the 1955 Railway Modernisation Plan that affected the North West was the drafting in 1959 of the 1-Co-Co-1 English Electric Type 4 diesel electric locomotives (later Type 40) to West Coast main line expresses after the first ten had gone to the Eastern Region, followed by the 'Peak' class 44, 45 and 46s on the Midland and L&Y lines, and much evident in the Manchester area on those former pre-Grouping railway routes. Later the Brush class 47s became the dominant diesel higher powered locomotive throughout BR. The electrification of the West Coast route with the overhead 25,000 volt ac system commenced between Manchester and Crewe in 1960, was extended to Nuneaton and from Crewe to Liverpool, and then to London with all services south of Liverpool, Manchester and Crewe on the Scottish route being fully worked by the 81-86 series of Bo-Bo electric locomotives throughout the 1960s. Between 1960 and 1968 the North West saw a complex mixture of steam, diesel and electric traction. In 1974, the route from Crewe to Glasgow was electrified with the new class 87 Bo-Bo electric locomotives replacing the diesel electric Class 50s (D400s) and the 1980s saw the APT tilting train experiment and in 1984, the high speed run of the APT from Euston to Glasgow in 3 hours 52 minutes, a time that a recent Pendolino attempted to beat and missed out by a few seconds. In the light of the decision to abort the APT following early train operation failures and problems, some HST 125 train operation commenced on the Midland lines and on the Euston–North Wales and Cross–Country routes. An updated version of the Class 87, the Class 90, entered service on the West Coast in 1986 and these held sway until the privatisation of British Rail which was phased in between 1994 and 1996. The West Coast route became Virgin Trains and saw the development and introduction of the Pendolinos which still twenty years later are the mainstay of the route now under the aegis of Avanti.

The non-electrified freight scene in the North West used the class '40', '45' and '47' diesels in addition to diesel locomotives of lesser power until privatisation, when the new freight company EWS (English, Welsh & Scottish Railway) brought over the General Motors class '66' diesel electrics from the USA in large numbers which still dominate the workings of several of the freight companies.

The interloper into the North West was the Great Western Railway with its northern route through Birmingham and Wolverhampton to Chester and Birkenhead, and its branch from Wellington even reaching right into Crewe itself, so that GW steam engines could be seen at the Gresty Road and Crewe South depots right up to 1965, even though the London Midland Region had assumed control of much of the Western Region's former Birmingham Division in the early 1960s. Before the Second World War GWR trains also ran into Manchester Exchange. Therefore a few photos of GW 'Bulldogs', 'Saints' and 'Stars' and later 'Castles' in addition to a trusty pannier and 'Prairie' tank take their rightful place in this book.

The map of the Lancashire and Yorkshire Railway on the tiled wall of Manchester Victoria station, 31 May 1996. (Harold D. Bowtell)

Preston station with an Aspinall 2-4-2 'Radial Tank' off a Blackpool train, c1920. (Real Photographs)

Manchester London Road station during a rebuilding of the main concourse area, 21 April 1960.

Manchester Ducie Street Goods Depot, 1954. (Brian K.B. Green)

Manchester Exchange station, c1966. (Rev. A.W.V. Mace)

Manchester Central station, 27 March 1962. The incoming train has a 'Black Five' cut inside for steam heating purposes. (G. Whitehead)

Manchester Airport station under construction, 30 May 1992. (Alan Gilbert)

Liverpool Exchange station, c1930. (Jim A. Peden Collection)

Liverpool Lime Street station, with 47246 on the 5.10pm express to Newcastle, 12 May 1979.

Liverpool Central station, October 1964 (closed in 1972). (J. Clarke)

Liverpool Riverside station, 3 August 1904. (Bob Miller Collection)

Liverpool Waterloo Goods Depot, taken from a railtour headed by 'Jinty' 47487, 13 June 1964. (Harold D. Bowtell)

Crewe station, with 'Caprotti' 44686 entering the platform with the *Pines Express,* 29 May 1952. Note Crewe station signal box within the station area. (R.S. Carpenter)

The north end of Crewe station with a typical mix of motive power found in the early 1960s, 7 July 1962. (G. Whitehead)

The north end of Crewe station during the six weeks closure for the remodelling, 29 June 1985. It was reopened a few days later by the local MP, Mrs Gwyneth Dunwoody, who had declared 'she would eat her hat' if it reopened on the scheduled date. She ate her hat.

Blackpool Central station, with station pilot, 42657 and 'Black Five' 45336 on the 6.30pm to Manchester Victoria, 2 September 1964.

Huddersfield station with an Aspinal 'Radial Tank', c1912.

Oldham Central station, looking east, 1925.

A postcard view of Littleborough station and town between Rochdale and Todmorden, c1910. Note an Aspinal 2-4-2T in the station and the scaffolding on the tall church spire.

A very early photograph of LNWR 2-4-0 No.24 *Sirocco* backing on to a train at Liverpool Lime Street, 1866.

L&Y Jenkins 0-6-0 No.224 at Clitheroe on the line from Blackburn to Hellifield, c1870. It was later rebuilt with a Hirst domeless boiler and cab in 1872 and was scrapped in 1893.

Barton Wright's standard passenger 4-4-0, 675, built by Sharp Stewart in 1881, at Southport after arrival with a train from Manchester, 1896. It was withdrawn two years later.

1512 *Henry Cort,* an LNWR Francis Webb Compound 2-2-2-2 of the 'John Hick' class at Crewe station with an Up express, c1895.

2063 *Huskisson,* an LNWR 2-2-2-0 Webb Compound of the 'Dreadnought' class, picking up water from Eccles troughs with a Belfast–Liverpool–London boat train, 1899. (Locomotive & General)

A 3-cylinder 2-2-2-0 Webb Compound on an Up express at Oxenholme, c1900. The line from Kendal and Windermere is seen coming in on the left.

Another unidentified Webb 3-cylinder compound 2-2-2-0 entering Hooton with a Chester–Birkenhead stopping train, c1900.

An 1874 Webb 'Precedent' 2-4-0, 1532 *Hampden,* at Windermere with the branch train for Oxenholme, c1905.

338, one of 160 2-4-2Ts built by the LNWR between 1890 and 1897 departing from Manchester Exchange, c1905. In the sidings is a GWR 2-4-0 that has arrived from Chester. It is 3232, the prototype of the last series of 2-4-0s designed by Dean built by Swindon in 1892.

1950 *Victorious,* a Webb 4-cylinder 4-4-0 of the 'Alfred the Great' class built in 1901 departing from Manchester London Road with an Up express, c1902. The class were later rebuilt with Joy valve gear similar to the 'Benbow' class between 1903 and 1907. It was further rebuilt as a 2-cylinder simple by Bowen-Cooke in 1922. (David Young Collection)

1423, an Aspinall L&Y 'Highflyer' 4-4-2 with 7ft 3in driving wheels, leaving Poulton with a Blackpool – Manchester express, 1904. It was one of the last constructed, in 1902, and was withdrawn as LMS 10338 in 1927.

One of Hughes' eighteen rail motors built for the L&Y between 1906 and 1911 at Watson Crossing on the Ripponden & Rishworth branch from Sowerby Bridge, a line that closed in 1929. This photograph was taken in 1908.

An unidentified LNWR 4-4-0 of the 1903 'Benbow' class, a 4-cylinder compound with Joy valve gear, on arrival with a stopping train at Manchester Exchange station, c1910.

1955 *Hannibal,* built in 1902 as a 4-cylinder compound of the 'Alfred the Great' class, rebuilt with Joy valve gear as a 'Benbow' at Crewe c1910. This was one of the few of the class that was not converted to the 2-cylinder simple 'Renown' class but was withdrawn as 3630 in 1923.

1520, a Hughes 'Dreadnought' class N1 4-6-0 built in December 1908 with Joy's valve gear, leaving Manchester Victoria with a train for Southport, passing LNWR 'Benbow' class 1971 *Euryalus,* 1910.

'Dreadnought' 1518 passing Manchester Exchange with a Manchester Victoria-'Blackpool Club' train, 1910.

1961 *Albemarle*, a Webb 4-cylinder 'Benbow' compound rebuilt as a 2-cylinder 'simple' engine of the Whale 'Renown' class in 1915, with a southbound express at Manchester London Road, c1919. It is attached to a Webb 2,000 gallon tender. It became LMS 5140 and was withdrawn in November 1927.

LNWR 'George V' class 1628 *Foxhound,* built in May 1911, at Edge Hill with a boat train from an Atlantic liner of the United States Lines. 5 April 1912.

1080, an Aspinall "A' class 0-6-0, built in 1891, passing Mirfield shed with a mineral train, c1912. Two more of the same class are under the coaling stage.

An unidentified Aspinall J4 4-4-0 with 7ft 3in driving wheels, passing Sowerby Bridge station, c1912. Note the complex structure with the underlying signals on the right.

311. an 0-6-0 saddle tank of class F15, built as an 0-6-0 tender engine in 1879 and rebuilt as a tank engine in 1893, with a ballast train at Watson's Crossing on the Rishworth branch, c1912. It was further rebuilt in 1916 and not withdrawn until 1938 as LMS 11365.

An Aspinall 2-4-2 class K2 'Radial Tank' slipping coaches from a Halifax–Manchester train at Rochdale, 9 October 1913. The first was constructed in 1889 and they continued in construction until 1910, by which time 375 had been built. Hughes rebuilt a number with Belpaire boilers and extended smokeboxes and the last forty built between 1905 and 1910 were constructed in this way. The locomotive photographed here was one of these.

731, one of ten 2-4-0s of class E7 of Ramsbottom's 'Newton' class, purchased by the L&Y from the LNWR in 1873, rebuilt with new boiler in 1889. This locomotive was rebuilt again in 1914 with a larger boiler and bogie tender with saloon attached for the Engineering Department. It was renumbered by the LMS 10000, painted red and not withdrawn until 1926. It is seen here at Manchester Victoria, 1914.

Two unidentified LNWR Whale 4-4-2 tank engines depart from Manchester London Road with a heavy commuter stopping train, c1920.

An LNWR 2-cylinder 'Precursor' 639 *Ajax,* built in 1904 at Euxton Junction with a Preston–Crewe stopping train, c1912. It was withdrawn in July 1928. (H.G. Tidey)

658, an Aspinall K2 'Radial Tank', built in 1899, at Huddersfield station with a stopping train for Leeds, c1912.

One of the experimental overhead line electric multiple units, 3501, built for the Holbrooke branch in 1913, at Tottington Junction, Bolton.

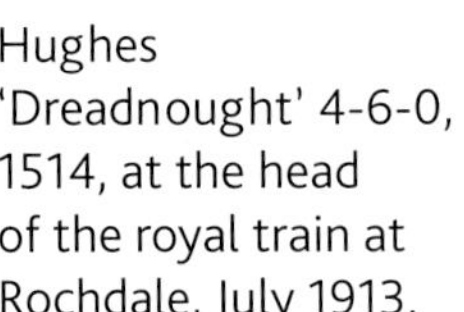

Hughes 'Dreadnought' 4-6-0, 1514, at the head of the royal train at Rochdale, July 1913.

A 'Precursor' 106 *Druid,* built in 1904 and superheated in December 1914, at Colwyn Bay on the Down *Irish Mail,* c1920. (Real photographs)

A small-boilered Aspinal 0-8-0 in Moston Cutting heading for Rochdale with a 'Jellicoe special' of coal for the royal navy at Scapa Flow, c1916. The 'cross' target in front of the chimney means that it has priority over all other traffic, even express passenger trains.

A superheated 'Precursor' No. 2 *Simoon,* at Colwyn Bay with a Down excursion train to Llandudno, c1920. (Real Photographs)

522, a 'Prince of Wales' 4-6-0 built at Crewe in June 1919, on the Up *Irish Mail* at Colwyn Bay, c1920. It was named *Stentor* in July 1922. (Real photographs)

The LNWR 'Claughton' class 4-cylinder 4-6-0 was introduced to Bowen-Cooke's design in 1913. Unnamed No.11 was built in July 1920 and is seen on a Down Scotch express approaching Preston the following year, 1921. (Locomotive & General)

The prototype 1913 built 2222 *Sir Gilbert Claughton*, the lone 'Claughton' converted to burn oil during the 1921 miners' strike, on a Down Glasgow express at Oxenholme, 1921. (H.G. Tidey)

1960 *Francis Stevenson,* built as an 'Alfred the Great' 4-cylinder compound in 1902, rebuilt as a 'Benbow' with Joy valve gear and finally rebuilt to the Whale designed 2-cylinder simple 'Renown' class in February 1918, renumbered 5153 by the LMS and withdrawn in October 1928. It is seen here at Stalybridge shortly after the last rebuilding, c1919.

A superheated 'Precursor', thought to be 564 *Erebus,* departing from Manchester London Road with a London express, c1920.

An unidentified Webb 'Precedent' 2-4-0 leaving Crewe with a train for Shrewsbury and the Great Western, c1920.

883 *Phantom*, a Webb 'Precedent' built in 1894, standing at Crewe ready to pilot a 'Claughton' on a northbound express, c1920. (Real Photographs)

1506, the first Hughes N1 'Dreadnought' constructed in June 1908, leaving Sowerby Bridge with a Manchester–Bradford via Halifax express, c1920.

1519, a Hughes 4-6-0 departing from Crewe with a northbound express, c1923. One result of the Grouping with George Hughes acting as the interim CME was the use of the large L&Y passenger engines on former LNWR routes.

123, an L&Y class '27' 0-6-0, constructed by Aspinall at Horwich in 1889, on a partially vacuum-fitted freight train at Horbury Junction, c1920. The train is signalled to the Barnsley branch.

1509. a Hughes 'Dreadnought', with a Manchester–Leeds train on Luddenfoot troughs, 1921.

Above: 700, an Aspinall 'Highflyer Atlantic' leaving Copley Tunnel near Sowerby Bridge with a Manchester–Leeds express, c1920.

Opposite above: An unidentified 'Highflyer Atlantic' departing from Manchester Victoria on Monsall Bank near Lightbowne with an express for Leeds and York, c1920.

Opposite below: 711, a 'Highflyer Atlantic' on a Manchester–Hull boat train at Middleton Junction, c1920. (G. Smith Collection)

LANCASHIRE & YORKSHIRE

1110, an Aspinall 4-4-0 of class J4, one of six rebuilt by Hughes in 1908/9 with superheating and high pitched boiler and Walschaerts valve gear, passing Manchester Exchange with a Fleetwood train, c1920.

An Aspinall 4-4-0, 985, of class J3, built by Beyer Peacock in 1888, pilots 'Highflyer' 1406 on a Manchester–York express at Middleton Junction, c1920. 985 was withdrawn as LMS 10109 in 1930 and 1406 as LME 10321 in 1931. (G. Smith Collection)

A pair of L&Y 4-4-0s, 980, an 1888 built 'J3' and 1108 an 1891 constructed 'J4', depart from Manchester Victoria with westbound train for Fleetwood or Blackpool, c1920.

A superheated L&Y class 'Q' (Hughes class '31') 0-8-0 introduced in 1912. No.216 was built at Horwich in 1916, It survived as LMS 12902 until 1947. on a train of coal empties near Hebden Bridge, c1922. (E.R. Wethersett)

An unidentified 2-4-2T , as rebuilt by Hughes from 1911 with superheater and Belpaire boiler, with an Manchester–Leeds express near Middleton Junction, c1920. (G. Smith Collection)

An Aspinall class '27', No.102 on the Low Moor breakdown train and crane, c1920. (Real photographs)

1113, a L&Y class '27' rebuilt in March 1911 with Belpaire boiler and extended smokebox, at Farington Junction with a Blackpool excursion, c1920. (H.G. Tidey)

An unidentified L&Y 'Q' 0-8-0 with a heavy goods train bound for Manchester at Middleton Junction, June 1919. (G. Smith Collection)

An Aspinall 0-6-0 on Healy Dell Viaduct near Facit on the Rochdale–Bacup branch, c1920. The viaduct is 105ft over the River Spodden.

1455, a small-boilered 0-8-0 at the head of a loose-coupled goods train at Middleton Junction, c1920. (G. Smith Collection)

An Aspinall designed 'J3' 4-4-0, constructed by Beyer Peacock in 1888, No.992 on a Manchester bound passenger train at Middleton Junction, c1920. It was withdrawn in 1932 as LMS 10115. (G. Smith Collection)

A 'Radial' 2-4-2T bound for Manchester Victoria and a Hughes 4-6-0 pass one another at Salford, c1920.

Atlantic 1398 leaving Manchester Victoria on Monsall Bank, between Thorps Bridge Junction and Smedley Viaduct, with a Liverpool–Leeds express, c1920.

An unidentified Aspinall 'Highflyer' leaving Sowerby Bridge Tunnel on the Halifax–Manchester route, c1920.

1221, a L&Y J4 4-4-0, one of two rebuilt in 1913 with Belpaire boilers, raised boiler pressure and extended smokebox, approaching Preston with a Blackpool excursion, c1922. It was withdrawn in 1926 as LMS 10166.

1357, a large-boilered 0-8-0 at Luddenfoot with a loose-couple goods train, 1921.

Crewe North shed, January 1923, with newly constructed Hughes 'Dreadnought' 1664 (later LMS 10435) with Walchaerts valve gear and superheater, and Claughton 5971 painted in the new LMS crimson lake livery and named *Croxteth*, June 1923. 5971 was rebuilt in 1930 as a Fowler 'Baby Scot' and renumbered 5500 and renamed *Patriot* as the precursor of the new class and the LMS war memorial engine.

1784 *Python,* a 'Precursor' built in October 1905, at Liverpool Lime Street, 5 April 1926.

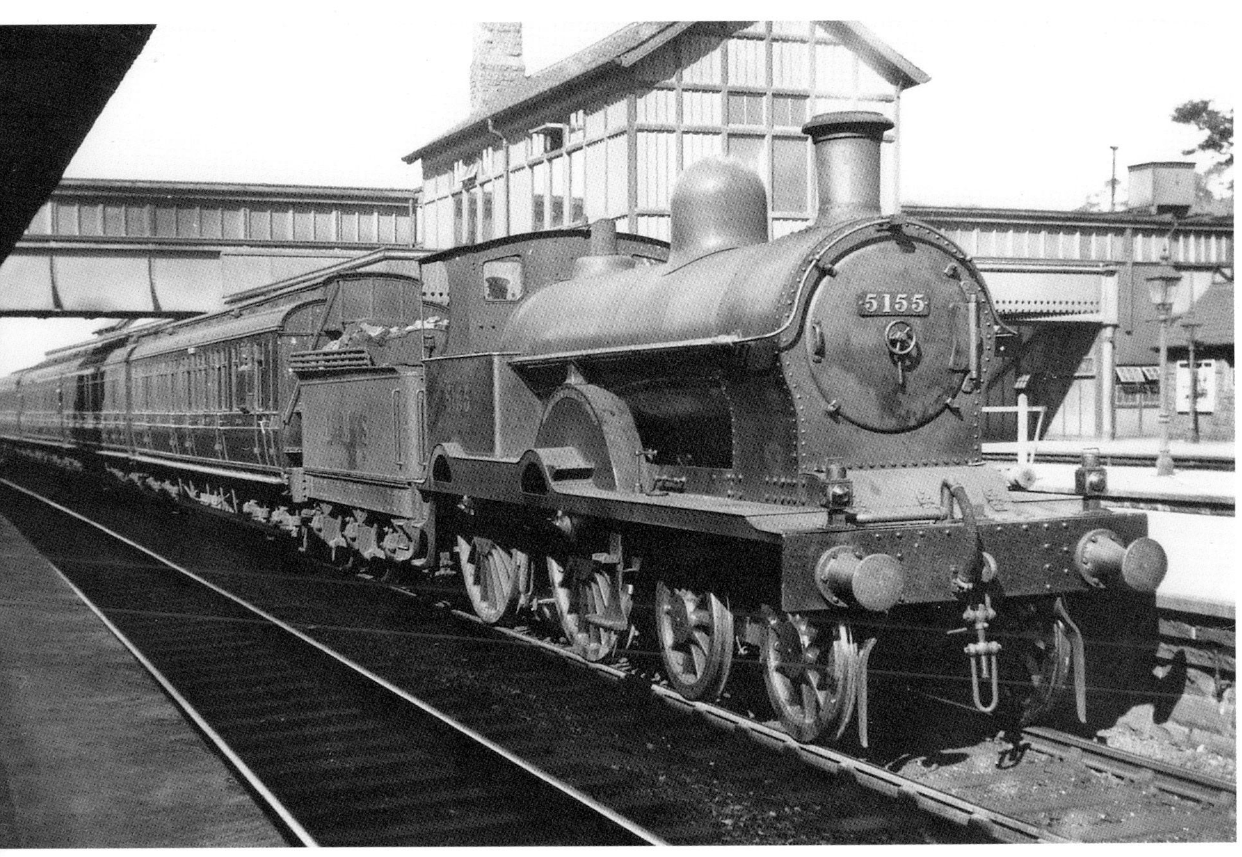

5155 *Irresistible,* formerly 1916, a Whale 2-cylinder rebuild of a Webb 4-cylinder compound 'Jubilee' class, on the 8.10am from Liverpool Central at Chinley station, 12 July 1928.

5020 *Delhi*, a Webb 'Precedent', formerly 1674 built in November 1890 and renumbered in June 1927, leaving Whitchurch with a stopping train to Chester via Malpas, c1928. It was withdrawn in November 1930. (C.J. Nevitt)

5092 *Violet,* a 'Waterloo' class 2-4-0 built as 763 in 1893 and withdrawn in 1930, arriving at Crewe with a stopping train from Shrewsbury, c1928. A Belpaire boilered 'Prince of Wales' 4-6-0 is on Crewe South shed in the background. A magnificent (and confusing?) array of signals on the gantry protecting the entrance to the station is operated from Crewe South Box.

Nine of the Webb 'Waterloo' class 2-4-0s (also known as 'Small Jumbos'), built between 1889 and 1896, were retained as Departmental engines for engineer saloon specials. 209 *Petrel* was initially renumbered 3496 and was based at Crewe between 1914 and 1932, when it was transferred to the Engineer South Wales before withdrawal a year later. It is seen entering Crewe station from the south, c1930. (Bill Potter)

The north end of Crewe station with a 'Patriot' leaving with a Plymouth–Manchester express, with 'Claughton and 'Experiment' 4-6-0s awaiting their next turn, c1930. The long footbridge from the station to Crewe North shed is seen in the background.

10614, a L&Y railmotor, on the Sowerby Bridge–Stainland branch which closed in 1929, seen here at West Vale station a couple of years previously.

12237, an Aspinall 0-6-0, on Luddenfoot troughs with a stopping train for Manchester, c1928.

Aspinall 2-4-2T 10807, formerly 1391 built in 1898, at Horwich station, c1928. I wonder what has caught the attention of the crew on the track! Or are they playing cards?

Claughton 5902 *Sir Frank Ree* takes water from Whitmore troughs as it heads the Down *Welshman* with wheeled containers loaded on flat wagons behind the tender, 7 June 1930. Note the water softening treatment equipment on the bank.

Three locomotives running in, tender-first, at Whitmore after overhaul at Crewe Works – Claughton 5925 *E.C. Trench*, superheated 'Precursor' 5282 *Champion* and Fowler 'Royal Scot' 6143 *Mail* (later *The South Staffordshire Regiment*), September 1929. (W. Leslie Good)

11111, a Baltic tank version of the Hughes L&Y 4-6-0, but not built until 1924, at Buxton, with a stopping train for Manchester, 1930. (E.R. Morten).This locomotive was scrapped in 1940 after a relatively short life, similar to its nine sisters, as it was really too powerful and uneconomic for stopping passenger trains and too unstable at speed for express work.

A trio of LMS power at Agecroft shed in 1930 – Baltic Tank 11115, an unidentified 'Crab' and Hughes 4-6-0 10452 (formerly L&Y 1681 built in July 1923).

'Royal Scot' 6139 *Ajax* (later named *The Welch* Regiment) on an Up express on Dillicar troughs, c1930. The photographer is, I suspect, about to get rather wet!

Another soaking? The fireman fails to withdraw the scoop in time as 5908's tender overflows after taking water on Whitmore troughs with the Down *Lancastrian,* c1930. 5908 was fitted with the larger boiler and smoke deflectors in December 1928. It was named *Alfred Fletcher*.

Claughton 5975 *Talisman* built in 1920 as LNWR No.12 and rebuilt with larger boiler in 1928 and entering Crewe with a Down express, c1932. It was withdrawn in May 1937.

Baltic Tank 11115 and Aspinal 2-4-2T 10751 (formerly 1318 built in 1896 and rebuilt in 1906), at Bolton shed, June 1936. (Bill Potter)

10901, an Aspinall 2-4-2T of class K3 built in 1911 with Belpaire firebox, extended smokebox and superheating piloting Fowler LMS 2P 4-4-0 584 on an eastbound express at Middleton Junction, c1932.

'Radial Tank' 10862 at Wakefield Kirkgate after arriving with the 3.05pm from Normanton, 29 June 1933.

Ex LNWR 'Precedent 2-4-0 5001 *Snowdon* (formerly 2191 built in 1875). It was renumbered 25001 in April 1934 to clear the number for a new 'Black 5' before withdrawal in October. It is seen here the previous year near Keswick.

As a contrast to the previous photograph taken the same year, new Stanier Pacific, 6201 *Princess Elizabeth* is seen moving away from Crewe station to go on shed at Crewe North, 1933.

6200 *The Princess Royal* at speed with an Up express on Brock troughs between Lancaster and Preston, 1934.

'Experiment' 4-6-0 5487 *Combermere* at Crewe station, 10 August 1934. An express is in the platform behind the barrier and a 'Royal Scot' is seen awaiting its next duty on the right.

Stanier's rebuilding of the high pressure locomotive *Fury* with tapered boiler that became the model for the subsequent rebuilding of the 'Royal Scots', seen here at Crewe Works in LMS crimson lake livery but before the naming, *British Legion,* 1935. (Real photographs)

The L&Y electrified the Liverpool–Southport line in 1904 and extended the electrification in the Liverpool area through to 1913 when the Manchester–Bury line was electrified. An LMS 1931 built electric unit is seen here at Manchester London Road, 2 May 1936. (Neville Fields)

The Great Western not only encroached onto the former LNWR system at Chester and Birkenhead but GW passenger and freight trains reached Crewe itself via the line from Wellington via Market Drayton, Audlem and the junction with the Shrewsbury line at Nantwich. 'Bulldog' 3445 *Flamingo* is departing from Crewe with a stopping train for Wellington, 1936. (Bob Miller Collection)

One of the early 'Stars' (identified by the large block casing over the inside cylinders) departing from Chester with a stopping train for Wolverhampton, a typical GW 'Siphon G' van in the formation, c1936. (F. Moore)

The Great Western at Manchester Exchange – new 'Dukedog' – a 'Duke' boiler on the frames of a 'Bulldog' - 3212 *Earl of Eldon* departing with the 1.50pm to Chester, May 1937. (Bill Potter)

One of the Aspinall 2-4-2Ts built in 1910 as 1543, rebuilt in 1922 with Belpaire firebox, extended smokebox and superheater, 10945, with a Leeds–Manchester stopping train on Luddenfoot troughs, 1937.

12321, an Aspinal 0-6-0 with extended smokebox, emerging from Lockwood Yews Hill Tunnel with a Huddersfield–Sheffield stopping train, 1936.

10827, an Aspinall 2-4-2T, formerly 183 built in 1898 and rebuilt in 1916 with lengthened bunker and water tanks, at Squires Gate with a stopping train from Blackpool Central for Lytham, 19 September 1937.

A busy scene at Norton Bridge as 4P Compound 1166 enters with an Up stopping train for Stafford and Rugby whilst a 'Royal Scot' awaits the road with a Down stopping service, 2 August 1937. (E.R. Morten)

LMS 4F 4338 on Luddenfoot troughs with Manchester bound empty stock for an excursion train, c1936.

Fowler 2-6-4T 2382 enters Buxton station with a stopping train from Manchester, 2 July 1938. (E.R. Morten)

Fowler 3MT 2-6-2T No.61 on Luddenfoot troughs with a Halifax–Manchester stopping train, 1937.

LMS compound 1048, built in 1924, at Great Rocks in the Peak District with a Derby–Manchester Central train, 24 July 1938. (E.R. Morten)

Stanier 3MT 2-6-2T No.151 at Macclesfield, 21 September 1938. It has set back into the middle road to allow an express to pass. (E.R. Morten)

LMS 2P 4-4-0 683 entering Southport with a semi-fast train from Manchester, June 1939. (E.R. Morten)

'Prince of Wales' LNWR 4-6-0, 25627 *Lewis Carroll* built in January 1914 and destined to be withdrawn just one month after this photograph was taken. It is at the head of a special excursion train for Manchester near Handforth, June 1936. (Bill Potter)

6137 *The Prince of Wales Volunteers (South Lancashire)* with the 3-coach portion of a London express for Penrith and Keswick climbing from Tebay to Shap summit under easy steam, 1938. (Photomatic)

6220 *Coronation* with the Down *Coronation Scot* on Shap Bank, c1938.

The departure of 6225 *Duchess of Gloucester* with a London express from Manchester London Road draws the eyes of the p-way gang, c1938.

6224 *Princess Alexandra* has steam to spare as it picks up water from Dillicar troughs with the Down *Coronation Scot*, 22 July 1938. (H.C. Doyle)

A break during the war years and 6223 *Princess Alice,* still streamlined but in filthy unkempt black livery, hauls a heavy 16-coach Glasgow–Euston express past Basford Hall out of Crewe, 13 July 1946. (Doug Darby)

G2a 9196 climbing Madeley bank with an Up goods train, 18 August 1946. (Doug Darby)

The last surviving 'Claughton', large boilered 6004, formerly 42 *Princess Louise,* at Tebay on an Up freight, 3 June 1947. It bears a train reporting number presumably from a previous passenger train working. 6004 was rebuilt with the larger boiler in 1928 but lost its name when Stanier Pacific 6204 received this name in 1935.

A Midland 3F 3723 shunting Gowhole sidings while a 'Crab' passes on an Up freight, 26 April 1947. (Doug Darby)

The pioneer 8F 2-8-0 48000 on an Up freight at Strines between Marple and Chinley, 7 August 1948. (Neville Fields)

An LNWR G1 0-8-0, 9187, in run down condition after the Second World War, at Stockport Edgeley shed, 1947. (Alan Gilbert)

Another G1, 49092, trundles through St Helen's with a freight, 28 May 1949.

A Stanier 3MT 2-6-2T, 106, at Thelwall on the 4.55pm stopping train from Manchester London Road to Warrington, 14 April 1948. (Doug Darby)

6223 *Princess Alice,* now 'defrocked' accelerates away from Preston past Barton & Broughton, with the Down *Royal Scot,* 1948.

An Ivatt 2MT 2-6-0, 6410, built in 1946, at Blackpool, c1947.

Ivatt's modernised Pacific for the post-war austere era, 46256 *Sir William Stanier,* at Crewe station with an Up express, 1948.

Ivatt's English Electric pair of 1,600hp diesels, 10001 leading and 10000, doublehead the Up *Royal Scot* at Winwick Junction, 8 September 1949.

In contrast, a LNWR 'Cauliflower Goods' newly given its BR number, 58439, ambles down the branch from Penrith with the 2.20pm (SO) to Keswick, 16 July 1949. (Doug Darby)

A new 'Black Five' with a self-weighing tender, 4986, awaits departure from Manchester Central with a stopping train for Derby, 13 March 1948. (H.C. Casserley)

Aspinal 0-6-0 12545 at Glodwick Road station with LNER C13 7421 on the 4.23pm railmotor to Guide Bridge, 27 April 1948.

5296 near Worsley with a Manchester–Carlisle partially fitted vacuum freight, c1948.

Rebuilt 'Scot', 46120 *Royal Inniskilling Fusilier* between Cheadle Hulme and Handforth with a Manchester–Euston express, c1950. (Tom Lewis)

Holbeck's ex-works rebuilt 'Scot' 46109 *Royal Engineer* slows for Sunday engineering work with a Manchester–Bristol and West of England express, c1950. It is travelling wrong line near Handforth. (Tom Lewis)

Another rebuilt 'Scot' 46124 *London Scottish* powers a Down express at Whitmore summit, 14 May 1952. (E.R. Morten)

Kentish Town's 45557 *New Brunswick* at Manchester Central with an express for St Pancras, while a GN C12 acts as station pilot in the bay platform, 17 April 1949. (Neville Fields)

A sad end for the 'Turbolocomotive'. 46202 is out of action at Edge Hill shed, 18 April 1950, shortly before its withdrawal and rebuilding into the ill-fated *Princess Anne.* (H.C. Casserley)

Back to the GWR again at Chester. 2915 *Saint Bartholomew* has arrived with an express from Paddington before reversal and the short hop onto Birkenhead, 10 May 1949. The impressive Chester No.6 Box is in the background.

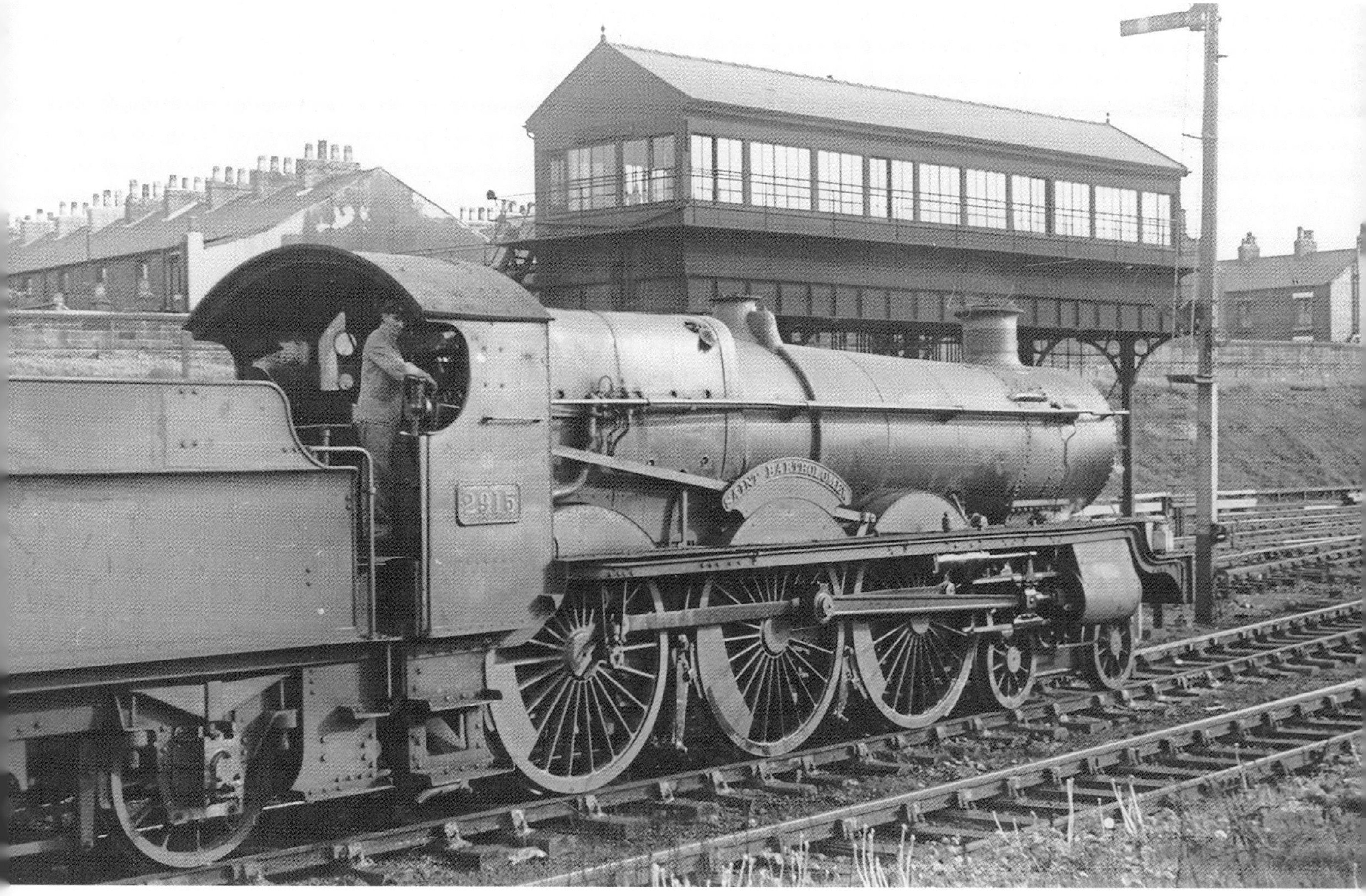

Shrewsbury's 4044 *Prince George* has just arrived at Shrewsbury with a West of England–Manchester express which will change to LMR motive power here, 12 May 1951. (David Young Collection)

Another 'foreigner' in the North West, ex Great Eastern D16/3 62535 with a Liverpool–Manchester train at Risley Moss, 19 March 1950. (Doug Darby)

'Crab' 42750 of Newton Heath on an Up stopping train near Cheadle Hulme, 27 March 1951. (Tom Lewis)

'Crab' 42725 and an electric unit at Heaton Park, looking north towards Prestwich and Bury, c1950.

'Jubilee' 45736 Phoenix rebuilt by Stanier with a larger tapered boiler after the fashion of the one designed for the rebuilt *Fury*, seen here on a Down express at Whitmore, 7 August 1950. (E.R. Morten)

Another photo of Kentish Town's 45557 *New Brunswick* on a Manchester–St Pancras express at Chapel-en-le-Frith, 16 May 1951. This photo is of special interest to me as I was 13 on this day and a week or so later while trainspotting in London travelled out to Cricklewood behind it on a Bedford stopping train, my first run behind a named LMS engine. (Neville Fields)

'Jubilee' 45553 *Canada* near Chorlton Junction with a southbound train, 1950. It is fitted with a small Midland tender still displaying LMS a couple of years after railway nationalisation. (Martin Shoults)

'Unrebuilt Patriot' 45529 *Llandudno* passing Longsight depot with a Manchester–Plymouth train, 9 June 1951.The excursion platform is on the left. (Tom Lewis)

44938 on an Up Midland route express at Heaton Mersey, 17 June 1951. (Brian K.B. Green)

'Crab' 42750 again passing Romiley with a train of loose coupled mineral wagons, 15 June 1951. (Tom Lewis)

46200 *The Princess Royal* in LMS lined black livery and the tender still inscribed 'LMS' nearly four years after nationalisation, seen on the Down *Midday Scot* at Standish Junction, September 1951.

'Crab' 42761 on a Nottingham–Belle Vue funfair and zoo excursion, at Great Rocks, 28 June 1952. (Brian K.B. Green)

Fowler 2-6-4T 42308 departing from Longsight on the 4.29pm Buxton–Manchester stopping train, 12 September 1952. (Brian K.B. Green)

'Unrebuilt Scot' 46156 *The South Wales Borderer* passing Cheadle Hulme station with a Manchester–Euston express, c1952. (Tom Lewis)

Blue 46228 *Duchess of Rutland* at Scout Green with the 10.40am Euston–Perth express, 28 May 1952. (E.D. Bruton)

Fowler 2-6-4T 42318 pilots GC 'Director' 62655 *The Earl of Kerry* on a Manchester–Chester stopping train past Hale, 12 February 1952. (Robert Fysh)

An other Fowler large passenger tank engine, 42319, on a Manchester–Buxton stopping train at Heaton Norris, c1953. (Jim Davenport)

The experimental 'Fell' diesel locomotive, 10800, working the 11.35am Manchester–Derby approaching Chinley North Junction, 28 June 1952. (Brian K.B. Green)

Two trains pass on the Liverpool Overhead Railway system, February 1954. (JWS/MLS Collection)

'Jubilee' 45555 *Quebec* rounds the curve off the Manchester line into Crewe with the Up *Mancunian*, 7 July 1952. (Tom Lewis)

One of the five 'Britannias' allocated initially to Longsight, 70033 *Charles Dickens,* near Pynton with the Down *Comet,* a Euston–Manchester express via Stoke, 23 March 1952. (David Young Collection)

A 'Jubilee' on the Transpennine route – 45556 *Nova Scotia* is working a Manchester–Newcastle football special over Saddleworth viaduct, c1952. (Jim Davenport)

45553 *Canada* working the 11.35am Manchester Central–Derby near Buxworth, 17 May 1952. (Brian K.B. Green)

'Unrebuilt Patriot' 45520 *Llandudno* passing Wilmslow with a Manchester–Plymouth express, 15 February 1952.

'Rebuilt Scot' 46126 *Royal Army Service Corps* on Dutton Viaduct (north of Acton Bridge) with a Euston–Liverpool express, c1953.

46151 *The Royal Horse Guardsman* at Madeley with a 15-coach Carlisle–Euston express, 22 July 1953. (Tom Lewis)

46149 *The Middlesex Regiment* coming off Stockport Viaduct into the station with a Manchester–Plymouth express, 22 August 1952. (E.R. Morten)

46101 *Royal Scots Grey* eases an Up express through the middle lines at Crewe station while Stanier Pacific 46248 *City of Leeds* waits for the road watched by a group of trainspotters, 1953. (Tom Lewis)

Camden's 46229 *Duchess of Hamilton* at Boars Head near Wigan with the *Royal Scot*, c1953. (Tom Lewis)

46221 *Queen Elizabeth* on the Up *Royal Scot* eases for the curve after Stafford station, c1953. (Tom Lewis)

Polmadie's 46224 *Princess Alexandra* passes slowly through Crewe with the Down *Royal Scot* with 46151 *The Royal Horse Guardsman* waits to follow it northwards, c1953. (G. Newall)

Crewe North's 46225 *Duchess of Gloucester* on the Up *Midday Scot* passing Victoria Colliery Sidings, near Standish, Wigan, c1953. (Tom Lewis)

Longsight's 70032 *Tennyson* working hard with a heavy Up express at Adswood, 3 April 1953. (Tom Lewis)

70043, then unnamed and fitted experimentally with Westinghouse brakes on the 2.05pm Manchester–Euston, 22 April 1954. The air brakes were later removed and the engine was named *Earl Kitchener.* (David Young Collection)

Surprise! A Great Western train at Stafford hauled by 5016 *Montgomery Castle*. This appears to be a Western Chester–Paddington express diverted from Wellington presumably because of some emergency line blockage on the GW route between there and Wolverhampton, November 1953. (Real photographs).

Birkenhead shed with Churchward 2-8-0 2822 and a Stanier mogul, 20 April 1954. (H.C. Casserley)

Another Birkenhead shed scene with GW pannier tank of the '2021' class, 2112., 20 April 1954. H.C. Casserley)

GW 'Large Priarie' 4125 at Birkenhead Woodside with a stopping train for Chester, 20 April 1954. (H.C. Casserley)

The GW Chester shed with 'Large Prairie' 5174, Collett 2-8-0, 3842 and a locally based 'Manor' 4-6-0, 6 September 1955. (A.C. Roberts)

Churchward 5ft 8in 2-8-0, 4704, departs from Morpeth Dock, Birkenhead with a fully vacuum-fitted freight for Paddington Goods and Smithfield, c1955. (Bernard Roberts)

GW pannier Tank 5719 and LMS Stanier mogul, 42964, amble over the River Dee past Chester Racecourse to Saltney Yard, c1955. (Brian K.B. Green)

'Unrebuilt Patriot' 45515 *Caernarvon* picks up water at Whitmore with an Up relief express, Summer 1955.

46115 *Scots Guardsman* (now preserved) accelerates the 10.15am Manchester–Euston express through Longsight station, 13 March 1955. (Neville Fields)

Bulleid designed SR diesel electric 10202 arrines on Crewe Noth shed off the 12noon Euston–Liverpool express with 46252 *City of Leicester* waiting to leave shed to resume haulage of the Liverpool express, 30 April 1955.

Woodhead route electric Bo-Bo 26001 on driver training pilots ER 'O4/3' 63835 on a Down freight at Torside, 15 May 1955. (Alan Gilbert)

26020, the Woodhead route electric exhibited at the Festival of Britain in 1951, on the Manchester portion of an express from Marylebone, at Dinting, April 1955.

Co-Co electric locomotive 27001 at Ardwick with a Manchester London Road–Marylebone express, 10 September 1954. (Brian K.B. Green)

A scene at Edge Hill shed, Liverpool, with 'Unrebuilt Patriot' 45515 *Caernarvon* and 'Jubilee' 45666 *Cornwallis* under the coaling stage, 25 May 1953. (R. Howarth)

44938 near Marple with a Manchester–Derby stopping train, 3 August 1953. (R.D. Pollard)

'Crab' 42760 with a Sheffield–Belle Vue excursion at Bullhouse on the Woodhead route, 19 April 1954. (Brian K.B. Green)

Aspinal 3F 0-6-0 52440 at Bacup with a stopping train for Manchester Victoria, 23 April 1954. (H.C. Casserley)

'Rebuilt Jubilee' 45736 *Phoenix* with a Manchester–London express near Heaton Chapel, c1956. (Ronnie Gee)

'Jubilee' 45734 *Meteor* assists a 'Rebuilt Patriot' on a Liverpool–Newcastle express near Droylsden, c1956. (Jim Davenport)

'Unrebuilt Patriot' 45520 *Llandudno* pilots a rebuilt version of the same class at Linthwaite with a Transpennine express, c1956.

46203 *Princess Margaret Rose* accelerates a Manchester–Euston express through Heaton Norris, 26 April 1956. (Tom Lewis)

46205 *Princess Victoria* picking up water at Whitmore with the Down *Red Rose* Liverpool express, 31 March 1956. 46205 had its inside valves operated by rocking shafts instead of the four independent sets of valve gear of the others of the class. (N.E. Preedy Collection)

Longsight's 70032 *Tennyson* passes Heaton Norris with a Euston–Manchester express, c1956. (Jim Davenport)

44716 entering Manchester London Road with a Birmingham–Manchester train, 1957. I had several runs behind this Rugby 'Black Five' in the winter of 1957 on a Rugby–Euston semi-fast from Willesden Junction when commuting from my gap year job at Old Oak Common.

'Crab' 42773 trundles a train on mineral empties southbound through Stockport Edgeley, 11 October 1957. (Ronnie Gee)

A Bowen-Cooke LNWR 0-8-0 G2a (rebuilt after 1936 from the 1912 built G1) saunters across the landscape with a lightweight goods train near Buxton, 12 June 1957. (Neville Fields)

Holbeck's 46103 *Royal Scots Fusilier* shunts Hamson's Sidings at Penrith, while BR Standard 2MT 78018 (now preserved) departs with a train for Keswick and Workington, c1958. (D. Cross)

Back to the Western Region! 4090 *Dorchester Castle* has just arrived at Shrewsbury with the Saturday *Cambrian Coast Express*, the photo labelled as 20 April 1957. However, 4090 was only rebuilt with 4-row superheating and double chimney (only the second to be converted) in April 1957. It became Old Oak's regular engine on the *Bristolian* during the weekdays for the following six months, working the 'CCE' on the Saturday mornings, and from its used state (note the bufferbeam) is more likely to have been taken in June or July 1957. (David Young Collection)

Dean's 1897 '2021' class of pannier tanks in the example of 2069 still survives shunting at Birkenhead, 30 March 1958. (Jim Peden Collection)

GW 'Large Prairie' 5103 with a Birkenhead–Chester stopping train, near Bebington, May 1958. (Jim .Peden Collection)

Fowler 2-6-4T 42319 at Ashley with the 4.27pm Manchester Central–Chester stopping train, 13 June 1959. (Ronnie Gee)

'Jubilee' 45733 *Novelty* south of Macclesfield with a Manchester–London via Stoke express, 9 May 1959. (Ray Farrell)

45552 *Silver Jubilee* on a westbound Transpennine express at Golcar, 22 April 1957. (Peter Hutchinson)

'Rebuilt Patriot' 45514 *Holyhead* departing from Manchester London Road with a stopping service to Crewe, running in after a Works overhaul, 1 April 1957. (Brian K.B. Green)

44935 at Davenport with the 12.50pm SO Manchester London Road–Buxton, 1 February 1958.

44714 runs into Crewe with a northbound relief train, c1958. (David Young Collection)

An old L&Y 1913 constructed third-rail electric multiple unit still operating at Bury (Bolton Street) with a stopping train for Manchester Victoria, June 1959. New stock was introduced in 1960.

L&Y EMU sets at Bury Bolton Street station in their last year of operation before replacement by new stock, 13 June 1959.

The signalman in Crumpsall Box watches a passing EMU en-route from Manchester Victoria to Bury, 1959.

L&Y electric unit M28505 at Woodlands Road Halt with a Bury–Manchester Victoria stopping train, 1959.

51343, an Aspinall 0-6-0 saddle tank, acting as the coal stage pilot at Newton Heath depot, 31 August 1959.

3F 0-6-0 52271 at Oldham Central station with the breakdown train which includes a 30-ton Sheldon crane, 4 April 1959. (Raymond Keeley)

The last L&Y class '25' 0-6-0, 52044, shunting at Darton on the Horbury Junction–Barnsley line, just a few weeks before its withdrawal in June 1959. It was saved from scrapping and subsequently after restoration, became a resident at the Keighley & Worth Valley heritage line.

'Crab' 42768 at Millers Dale with a Down pick-up goods train, 17 August 1959.

46201 *Princess Elizabeth* near Acton Grange with a heavy Up express for Euston, c1959. (Tom Lewis)

A filthy 46209 *Princess Beatrice* climbing to Shap summit with a Liverpool–Glasgow express, August 1960. (P.H. Groom)

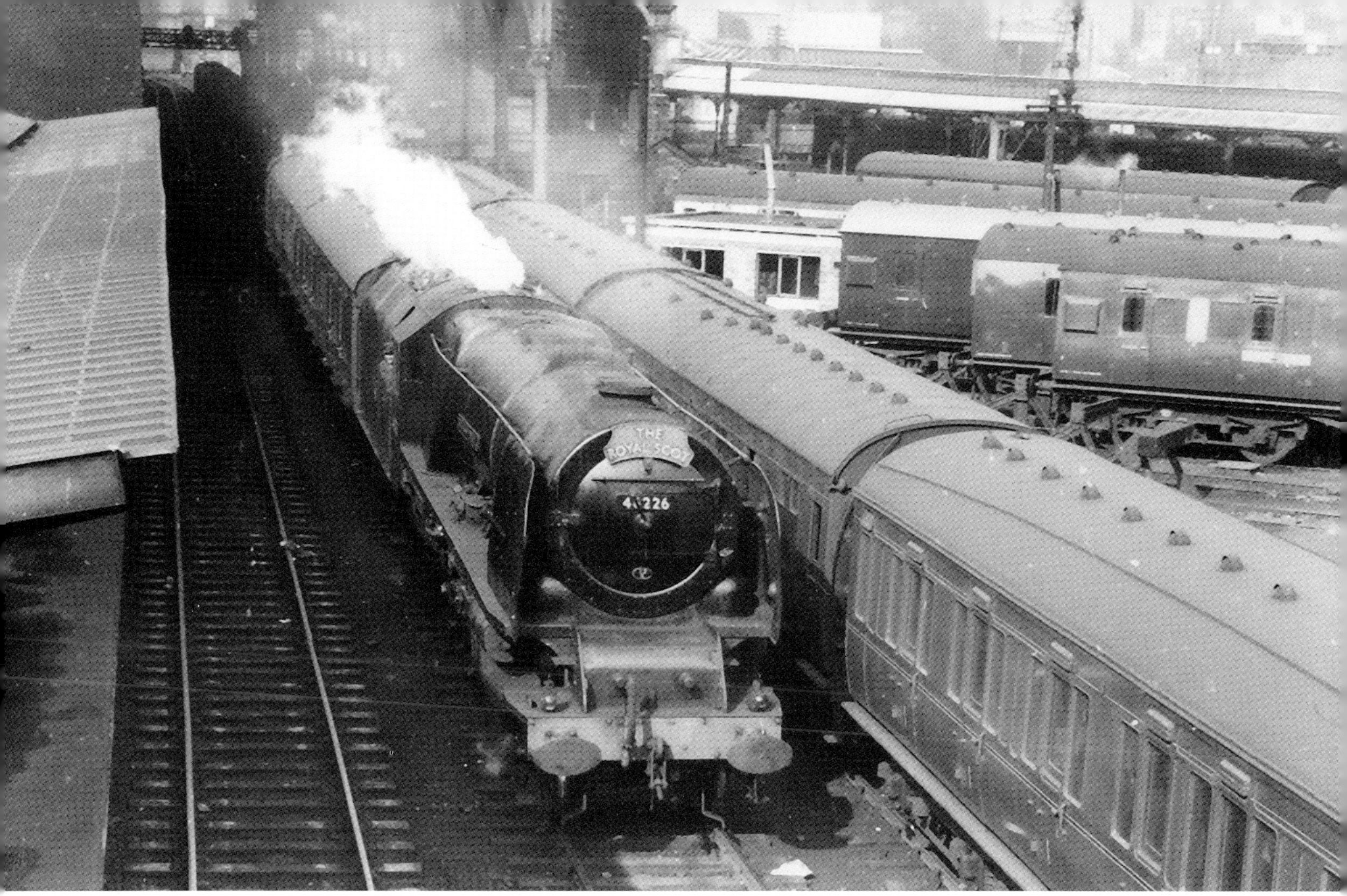

Carlisle Upperby's 46226 *Duchess of Norfolk* slips through Preston station with the Up *Royal Scot,* 13 March 1959. To the right is the former East Lancs station, now a car park. (A. Vaughan)

A Barton-Wright 0-4-4 tank engine of 1877 design still used as a stationary boiler at Blackpool North, 4 August 1960. Most members of the class were withdrawn between 1908 and 1912, but No.14, built by Sharp Stewart in 1886, was the last withdrawn in 1921 and used thereafter for carriage warming at Blackpool while others did similar duties at Low Moor, Liverpool, Southport and other centres. No.14 was the last survivor of these. (Bill Potter)

L&Y 3F 52270 shunting New Hey goods yard on the Oldham loop line, overlooked by St Thomas's Church, 28 May 1960. (Richard Greenwood)

51497, a L&Y saddle tank, on the 8.35amHartford Sidings–Brewery Sidings trip goods used to get the Royton pilot back to its depot. (B. Hilton)

A pair of Aspinall 3Rs, 52159 and 52165, at Royton Junction, taken from the Holyrood Street bridge, c1960. (Jim Davenport)

'Crab' 42748 with a train of loose couple mineral wagons at Hazel Grove, 7 January 1961. (Alan Gilbert)

'G2a' 49104 pulls away from Preston station with an Up freight while 75048 waits in the platform with a Manchester train, 1961. (W.H. Ashcroft)

70048 *The Territorial Army 1908–1958* with an Up semi-fast train at Leyland, 1 July 1961. (I.G. Holt)

Bank Hall's unnamed 'unrebuilt Patriot' 45517 at Pendlebury on the 10.30am Liverpool Exchange–York, May 1961. (Peter Reeves)

The same 'Patriot', 45517, tender-first hauling a Bridlington–Oldham relief train, near Shaw, 24 June 1961. (I.G. Holt)

46225 *Duchess of Gloucester* on a Down express at Boar's Head, 20 May 1961. (Ray Farrell)

Camden's 46244 *King George VI* with the 3.45pm Euston–Glasgow *Caledonian* at Vale Royal between Winsford and Hartford, 8 August 1960. (John Hilton)

46244 *King George VI* on the 1.05pm Liverpool–Euston near Action Bridge, 18 June 1960. (John Hilton)

The Ivatt built 'Duchess', 46256 *Sir William Stanier,* on the 11am Birmingham New Street–Glasgow at Winwick Junction, 18 March 1961. (Alan Gilbert)

Two new A/C electric locomotives, E3017 (later class 81) and a sister running in after construction, with a Manchester–Birmingham service at Stockport Edgeley station, July 1961. The station building in the background houses the Manchester Locomotive Society's clubrooms on the 1st floor.

'Caprotti Standard Five' 73133 departing from Chester with an excursion for the North Wales coast, 22 July 1962.

An unidentified Fowler 4F 0-6-0 with a late running parcels train near Disley between Stockport and Buxton, 3 March 1962.

Stockport Edgeley station with Fowler 2-6-4T 42316 ready to shunt the Palethorpe's Sausages van, ready to return to Birmingham the next morning, Fairburn 2-6-4T 42084 and E3004 (later 81004),12 July 1962. (Gerald Harrop)

'Rebuilt Jubilee' 45735 *Comet* near Weaverham between Winsford and Hartford on a Down relief train for the Lakes District, 5 August 1962.

46200 *The Princess Royal* with an RCTS special railtour train departing from Chester for the North Wales coast overtakes 45142 on a Chester–Wolverhampton train, 22 July 1962.

Kingmoor's 46203 *Princess Margaret Rose* passing Euxton Junction with the 12.46pm Crewe–Carlisle parcels train, 24 February 1962.

Two 'Princess Royals' in store at Liverpool Edge Hill depot – 46208 *Princess Helena Victoria* and 46204 *Princess Louise*, 1962. (D.I.D. Loveday)

44712 departing from Chester with the 9.10am to Manchester, 27 July 1963. (D. Frost)

'Crab' 42748 shunting at Disley, being called back to the Goods Yard in the severe winter of 1963, 16 February 1963. (Wallace Sutherland)

Lostock Hall's 45592 *Indore* at Bolton Trinity Street station with a train for Preston, 20 July 1963. (Ray Farrell)

'Rebuilt Jubilee' 45736 *Phoenix* climbing past Shap Quarry with the 10.35am Glasgow–Blackpool on a wet Saturday of the Glasgow Fair fortnight, 18 July 1964.

45590 *Travancore* on a Blackpool–Manchester relief train near Leyland, May 1964. (Photomatic)

45552 *Silver Jubilee* in its latter days, complete with yellow stripe prohibiting from going south of Crewe, on a Down vacuum-fitted freight near Hest Bank, 15 August 1964. (Peter Hutchinson)

Carlisle's 46136 *The Border Regiment* leaving Blackpool Central with a return 2.55pm Blackpool Lights excursion to Paisley, 16 July 1963. Another 'Scot' waits to follow. (F. Dean)

Kingmoor's 46166 *The London Rifle Brigade* at Skew Bridge with an Up train of gas tanks, 16 May 1964. (Alan Gilbert)

Edge Hill's 46229 *Duchess of Hamilton* on the Down *Lakes Express,* at Standish, 10 August 1963. I was on board in the first coach, travelling from Euston to Preston.

Upperby's 46238 *City of Carlisle* at Standish on a relief Euston–Glasgow express, 13 July 1963.

46228 *Duchess of Rutland* at Standish with a Down parcels train, 23 May 1964.

46256 *Sir William Stanier* at Golbourne with a Down parcels train, 3 May 1964. (Richard Greenwood)

46256 *Sir William Stanier* at Crewe backing onto the last railtour turn to and from Carlisle, 26 September 1964. The remaining 'Duchess' pacifics had all been withdrawn in the previous few weeks. The new motive power is visible in the station – an AC electric and a class 40 diesel electric locomotive. (Neville Fields)

70024 formerly named *Vulcan* and based at Cardiff Canton, transferred to Kingmoor and hauling a lightweight parcels train on Brock troughs, 16 October 1965. Note the scarcity of cars on the newly built M6! (Neville Fields)

A far cry from its days as *William Shakespeare* on the *Golden Arrow,* unnamed 70004 is hauling a partially braked freight at Winwick Quay, 27 March 1965. (Neville Fields)

44717 on a return Blackpool–Glasgow excursion train that was 'up for the lights' at Oxenholme, 27 September 1965. (Alan Gilbert)

44934 with a westbound freight at Mirfield, 30 April 1966.

The last steam hauled royal train? 45562 *Alberta* with the 1948 royal train stock after stabling overnight near South Stainley in 1967.

8F 48556 on an Up goods at Farington Junction, 26 May 1967.

48252 with a train of empty mineral wagons coming from the Garston Docks direction eastbound towards Stockport at Skelton Junction, 29 December 1967. (Neville Fields)

The pioneer 8F after withdrawal at Stockport Edgeley shed, 16 April 1967. (Alan Gilbert)

The last year of steam working took place in the North West and was celebrated, if that is the right word, by many rail enthusiast special trains. One on which the author participated is this railtour hauled by 'Caprotti Standard Five' 73134 and the last surviving Walschaerts 'Standard Five', 73069. It is seen at Greenfield on the Birmingham–Huddersfield leg of the tour, 20 April 1968. (Alan Gilbert)

73069 tackles the fearsome gradient with four hoppers of ballast at Chequerbent towards Bolton Goods Depot, 6 June 1968. It will have split the load as the full load of ballast would have caused a stall. (Neville Fields)

Very nearly the end of scheduled steam on British Railways – 45156 stripped of its name *Ayrshire Yeomanry* – at Stockport at the start of a railtour, the 10.01am to Carnforth, 4 August 1968. (Alan Gilbert)

The end – 45156's fire is extinguished at Rose Grove shed on the last day of steam working on BR, 8 August 1968. (Ray Farrell)

'Peak' class D158 at Stockport Tiviot Dale on the 9.25am Manchester–Sheffield, 30 November 1966. (G.Neve)

D166 at Holroyd Junction Huddersfield with a Liverpool bound TransPennine express, c1966.

English Electric Type 4, later class '40', D348 on a Castleford–Blackpool North excursion approaching Hall Toryd Junction, Todmorden, 29 May 1966. (Alan Gilbert)

D232 *Empress of Canada* leaving Oldham Mumps with the 10.30am to Blackpool Wakes special train, 19 June 1971. (Peter Hutchinson)

D226 departing from Crewe towards Basford Hall Junction with a southbound van train, 17 February 1970.

A pair of class '50s', D406 and D407 on 1M18 at Moore on a southbound express which they will work to Crewe where electric traction will take over, 4 May 1972. The bridge over the Mersey Ship Canal at Acton Grange can be seen in the background. (John Hilton)

The pioneer electric locomotive for the Woodhead line electrification, 26000 *Tommy*, is seen stored at Bury, 2 April 1972.

AC Bo-Bo electric 85004 entering Liverpool Lime Street with the empty stock for the 5.10pm express to Newcastle, 12 May 1979. (Alan Gilbert)

A class 306 EMU with the 11.30am Manchester–Hadfield crossing Dinting Viaduct, 17 April 1981.

WCML class 86/2, 86221 on an Up express and APT 37003 on a test run at Crewe station, 1984.

Brush Type 4, 47401, on the 11.03am Liverpool Lime Street to Newcastle at Manchester Victoria, 3 October 1987. (Alan Gilbert)

86252 *The Liverpool Daily Post* on the 12.05pm Glasgow–Euston passing 81006 on the 2.18pm Holyhead–Euston at Stafford, 16 June 1985.

86226 *Royal Mail Midlands* and a train of InterCity Mark III stock entering Stockport station with a Euston Manchester express, c1988.

81009 on an Up Freightliner train approaching Manchester Oxford Road station, 12 August 1989.

37239 and 37431 on the 2.23pm Bolton–Cardiff parcels train at Crewe station, 18 August 1990. (Alan Gilbert)

86411 *Airey Neave*, renumbered from 86011 after being re-bogied and resprung for 100mph running in 1984 at the head of the 1pm Manchester–Euston, with a 'Pacer' on the 11.20am Wigan–Cheadle Hulme at Manchester Piccadilly, 30 April 1990. Note the electric loco is being attached ahead of the Driving Van Trailer that normally headed London bound WCML InterCity expresses at this time.

A London express headed by a DVT and a Cross-Country HST unit at Crewe station, 6 December 1991. (Jim Davenport)

A freight business electric B0-Bo 90041 unusually heading an Up football special from Liverpool into Crewe with an InterCity class 90 and 87 stabled in the bay platform behind, 18 November 1990.

A Channel Tunnel TGV 373.3012 on the only occasion that it entered Manchester Piccadilly station on a test run from Bletchley, as 47805 departs with the 9.17am Cross-country train to Paddington via Birmingham and Reading, 20 February 1998. Some redundant units were being tested for use in this country as they were being replaced by French built 374 units and were used for a time on the East Coast Main Line, but despite this test, never on the WCML. (Alan Gilbert)

Royal Mail EMU 325.003 entering Manchester Piccadilly station, 15 August 1996.

AM 10 EMU 305515 at Platform No.1 Manchester Piccadilly with the 2.25pm to Hadfield, 7 August 1997.

EMU 323230 on the 2.42pm Manchester Piccadilly-Macclesfield at Bramhall, 31 March 1997.

A class 322 EMU ECS passing Cheadle Hulme station, en route to Alderley Edge sidings before forming a Wilmslow–Manchester Airport train, 18 May 1999.

Two EWS locomotives at Crewe - Bo-Bo electric loco 90031 *The Railway Children Partnership* and Brush 47773 *The Queen Mother*, 13 September 2003. The class 90 was named at the Old Oak Common Open Day in 2000 by members of the 'Railway Children' theatre cast after the charity founded by the author in 1995 and supported by the UK railway industry and the Manchester Locomotive Society.

A new Voyager 'tilting' diesel unit 221110 at Manchester Piccadilly station, a local 323 unit on the right, 7 March 2002.

A new Virgin Pendolino unit on a driver training trip at Bramhall, 2 June 2004. (Alan Gilbert)

The rear of the 2.5pm Manchester Piccadilly–Euston Pendolino 390052 and via Stoke and the freight business 90040 *The Railway Mission* on a Down express at Stockport station, 14 July 2005. The Pendolino unit has now been strengthened from 9 to 11 cars and has been renumbered 390152.

One of the class 57 'Thunderbird' diesel electric locomotives equipped to be attached to Pendolino units, 57301 *Scott Tracey* is detached from Pendolino 390036 at Crewe after working from Chester with a London train, 23 September 2006.

Freightliner's General Motors class '66', 66952 at Warrington Bank Quay with an Up Freightliner hopper train, 19 April 2007.

Merseyrail electric unit 308134 at Bidston with a West Kirby–Liverpool James Street train, 23 August 2007. (Neville Knight)

Silver liveried 67029 *Royal Diamond* with the ECS of the *Northern Belle* Pullman excursion train, at Altrincham, 23 July 2009. The overheads wires for the Manchester Metrolink trams are to the right background. (Norman Spilsbury)

Two EWS General Motors '66' class Co-Co diesel electric locomotives at Dove Holes Quarry Sidings, Peak Forest, 29 August 2012. (Joe Lloyd)

Colas Rail's 66849 *Wylam Dilly* passing Levenshulme with the regular Carlisle–Chirk log train, 19 July 2013. The same company's 66850 was named after this book's author at the Network Rail Plant Exhibition at Long Marston in 2013. (Alan Gilbert)